CONTENTS

Title Page	1
Chapter 1	3
Chapter 2: Balancing your assets	5
Chapter 3: Mutual funds	9
Chapter 4: Stock investing	23
Chapter 5: Using retirement accounts to your advantage	30
Chapter 6: From broke to millionaire plan in 15 years	37

HARVESTING WEALTH

Financial savvy to make you the boss of money

J.P. Medson

CHAPTER 1

Investing is good for you

Money is important. Average people spend over 13% of their entire lives working for a paycheck. You certainly know above average people who work day and night because they are trustworthy, dependable and not rich enough. Perhaps you're above average and happen to be reading this on one of your timed breaks. You also know below average people who put more effort into pursuing personal goals rather than making their bosses rich. Money is a common language that spans cultures to be used for exchanging goods and services. The world has a lot of money but almost none of it is in your pocket. In fact, most wealth is tied up in the businesses we work for and buy things from. Investing allows you to take a stake in any public company and profit from its successes, like a boss. While great businesses become more valuable over time, cash loses its value through inflation (**Fig. 1**). If you remember when gas cost $1 per gallon, you lived in an era when $1 was more valuable than it is today. That same dollar invested would have grown to $9 today, outpacing inflation by more than 4-fold. Simply put, investments are more valuable and powerful than cash. This book will show you how to invest for long-term growth, defined as a period of time equal to or greater than 10 years. The longer you invest, the more money you make. The last chapter details a plan for transforming your non-existent net worth into a respectable number. Savvy and disciplined investors will be able to use this information to acquire generational-spanning wealth by utilizing the public stock market at everyone's disposal. Rather than worrying about making money for your boss, become an investor to profit in the successes of the world's most innovative businesses. This book is a guide for people who really need to start investing to obtain long-term financial stability or for those wishing to optimize the performance and benefits of various retirement accounts. By following the plan laid out in Chapter 6, you will have the option of retiring from the workforce after approximately 15 years. Just think- people who retire at age 50 will spend 20,000 fewer hours working for a boss than those who retire at age 60! Time is one of the most valuable assets in all of humanity and financial stability will certain give you more time to pursue your personal interests.

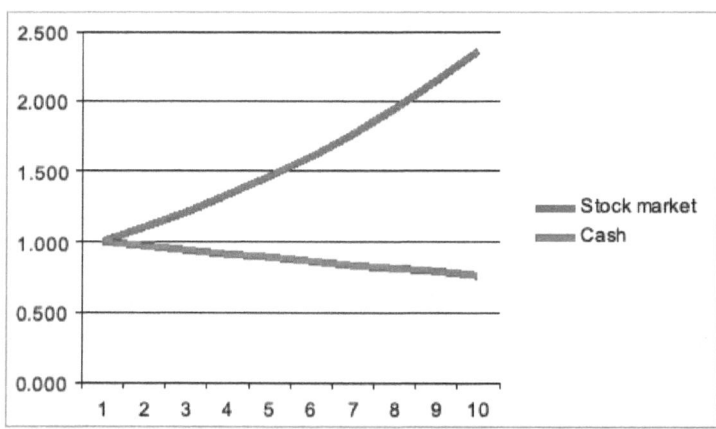

Figure 1. Value/Purchasing Power vs. Time

CHAPTER 2

Balancing your assets

Historically, investments in United States stocks increase in value by an average of 10% per year. This, coupled with steady decreases in the purchasing power of cash, means that stocks are more valuable than cash. Growing your wealth depends on investing your cash into businesses. Nonetheless, people have several hindrances to investing, often citing the risk, lack of knowledge or inability to choose a trustworthy financial consultant. Always remember that, despite the term, a stock-broker is not supposed to make you broke by charging hefty fees. The fact that very few brokers are geniuses means you can invest just as well with little to no experience if you follow my guidelines. Nowadays, it is incredibly easy to open online investment accounts from established institutions, and better yet, you don't need to interact with financial consultants who would rather put your money in their pockets. This guide is intended to give inexperienced newbies the information, confidence and guidance needed to take concrete steps towards building a powerful sustainable investment portfolio with unlimited potential. The overall composition of a portfolio is described in this chapter.

One of the most common investment terms is "**asset allocation**." Asset refers to one of the several different types of investments while allocation means the fraction of your total investments (based on value) that are held within each asset. This book primarily focuses on stocks, with other types of assets including bonds, cash, real-estate, and cryptocurrencies. Any possession worth monetary value can be considered an asset; however, only the assets that increase in value are viable investments. Therefore, cash is not an investment and its primary function is to be used for daily living expenses. Extra money that is not needed for this should be converted to an investment such as stocks, real-estate or bonds. In the case of unforeseen emergencies, stocks can easily be cashed out from non-retirement accounts to help pay the bills, hopefully after some capital gains have accrued.

Bonds are not purchased but rather are monetary loans that you provide to the government or various corporations with their promise to repay in full along with additional interest in the form of dividends. The purpose of bonds is to provide a source of income from these dividends to pay for your living expenses. While the value of bonds generally increases with the rate of inflation, you have to already be rich for them to play a significant role in your portfolio. During the process of becoming rich, stocks that increase in value over time can be gradually converted into bonds to provide the dividend income you will need to live off. This becomes an important consideration for portfolio rebalancing, as bonds are usually very good at preserving your principle from depreciation over short periods of time. Since stock prices are known to heavily fluctuate in periods of 1 to 5 years, bonds are more stable since their dividend rates are determined on the day of purchase. As with any other investment vehicle, a variety of bonds can be purchased in the form of mutual funds, which are managed by people trained in trading the asset. In other words, the fund managers are working for you!

Overall, bonds are advantageous during periods when stock prices are slumping since most of your investment value will be preserved and dividends will be reinvested into the purchase of more bonds at lower prices. The problem is, no one can predict what the market will do tomorrow. When stocks hit a recession, the allocation of bonds in your portfolio increases. When it reaches a certain predetermined level, you should rebalance by converting some of your bonds into stocks to achieve your desired asset allocation. That way, when the market eventually recovers and soars to new highs you will reap more of the gains! Conversely, market upswings will result in your stock allocation becoming overweight. In this case, it may be time to put your stocks on a diet and lock in some of your winnings by converting them to bonds until the next market downturn. This is the rationale for **portfolio rebalancing**. To make it work (for you), you simply have to monitor your asset allocation and adjust it when necessary. Starters can do this by entirely using mutual funds from their favorite investment family, while folks with larger portfolios will accomplish this with individual stocks. The following tables represent the benefits of portfolio rebalancing and asset allocation during three-year periods that include drastic market downturns (**Fig. 2**).

Scenario 1 Market depreciates 30% in one year and gains 40% following two years				Scenario 2 Market gains 30% in one year and depreciates 40% following two years		
Stock:Bond ratio	87:13	100:0	Stock:Bond ratio	87:13	100:0
Original balance	$100,000	$100,000	Original balance	$100,000	$100,000
Year 3 with rebalancing	$100,500		Year 3 with rebalancing	$83,200	
Year 3, no rebalancing	$99,210	$98,000	Year 3, no rebalancing	$81,810	$78,000

Figure 2. Advantages of holding a portion of your portfolio in bonds are realized during periods of stock market depreciation when funds are appropriately rebalanced.

As you can see, having bonds in the portfolio and rebalancing were beneficial in these worst-case scenarios. Investors that are closer to financial independence and have a shorter time frame will have a larger proportion of bonds compared to broke new investors with a long time frame. From my experience, the best strategy for growth is to use the asset allocation that historically has provided 9% returns each year: 87% of your portfolio in stocks and 13% in bonds that currently pay 2.4% interest in the form of dividends each year. This was determined using the following formula:

Stock allocation: 87% x 10% return = 8.7% annual gain
Bond allocation: 13% x 2.4% return = 0.3% annual gain
9.0% total annual gain

You can adjust this formula to whatever interest rate you are getting from bonds. Thus, bonds are used to not only provide income, but also to preserve the value of your investments during market downturns. For the latter purpose, all dividends should be reinvested to purchase more shares of your bond fund. Higher bond yields will allow you to allocate a larger portion of your assets into this class. For instance, if yields doubled to 4.8%, then you could have 19% of your assets held in this asset and still achieve a 9% return on average. During its growth phase, your portfolio should be rebalanced every year in order to stay on track for the 9% average annual return. This will prevent against significant deviation from the 13% bond allocation and protect against volatility. Of course this allocation can be adjusted to meet your needs. Keep in mind that investments that increase by 9% per year will double in value every 8 years! If you are already financially independent and can live on bond interest from a smaller allocation and want to water the seeds for your offspring, then use the allocation that has the best probability of meeting your goal. For instance, if your annual expenditures are $80,000 and you want to primarily live off bond interest, you will need to invest about $4 million into bond funds to achieve this goal without cashing out your principle investment.

While stocks and bonds are sufficient for your investment portfolio, some individuals dive into real-estate since it is another asset that increases in value over time. Real-estate, such as houses, apartments, land, can be purchased outright or in the form of real-estate investment trusts (REITs), which are similar to a mutual fund.

CHAPTER 3

Mutual funds

Most people do not own investments. If you take a poll, only a few reasons exist for this: 1) everything they earn is required to cover living expenses, 2) they don't know how to start, and 3) they place a high priority on protecting assets from losing any value during a recession that may or may not happen in the near or distant future. Fixing reason 1 is outside the scope of this book, and you simply need to land a job that allows you to invest a portion of your income. People who have fallen under reasons 2 and 3 certainly stand to benefit from reading ahead. Getting started in investing is quite simple and you do *NOT* need a money manager to pocket the earnings that your partially-owned companies have worked tirelessly to provide you. In fact, if the title money manager was based on a someone's performance rather than educational degree, everyone who purchases mutual funds may consider themselves to be a money manager. This is because people with investible assets can actually outperform professional portfolio managers by doing very little in the form of setting up periodic payments and waiting.

The stock market consists of thousands of publicly traded companies. On average, the price of American stocks increase by 10% each year. When you analyze individual stocks, however, prices may deviate from the overall market average. Some companies do well and others not so well based on their earnings, supply and demand. Rather than picking a few stocks and hoping it turns out well, the best way to *BEGIN* your investing career is to purchase small pieces of several companies that approximate the performance of the overall market. This will ensure your best chance of achieving a 10% annual return on investment. Mutual funds provide you with this opportunity. Large financial firms have managers that accumulate many different stocks into their portfolio. The ratio of these different stocks will determine the overall value and performance of their portfolio, termed a **mutual fund**, with investors like us buying pieces of it. Each fraction, or **share**, of the mutual fund contains the entire repertoire of stocks that have been accumulated by the fund manager in the same relative proportions (**Fig. 3**). In addition to providing buyers with exposure to a broad array of stocks, many mutual funds have low managerial fees allowing for most of the earnings to go into your pocket! The first mutual fund was the Massachusetts Investors Fund, starting in 1924. Today it has approximately 70 stocks with a combined value of $5.7 billion. Most of these are large American companies. On January 8, 1930, anyone could have bought a share of the Massachusetts Investors Fund for $6.97. Today's share price is a little over $31; however, the one purchased in 1930 is much more valuable today than $31. Dividends and capital gains paid by the fund to its investors are typically reinvested to purchase more shares. For example, today's annual dividend and capital gain payout of $3.70 per share is worth more than 10% the price of one share. Taking these reinvestments into account along with steady increases in share prices resulted in this mutual fund increasing in value by 1,800-fold between the years 1930 and 2019. Thus, the original $6.97 share would have sprouted into 400 shares worth over $12,000 today. If anyone asks you to prove that time is money, you can point to this or a similar example.

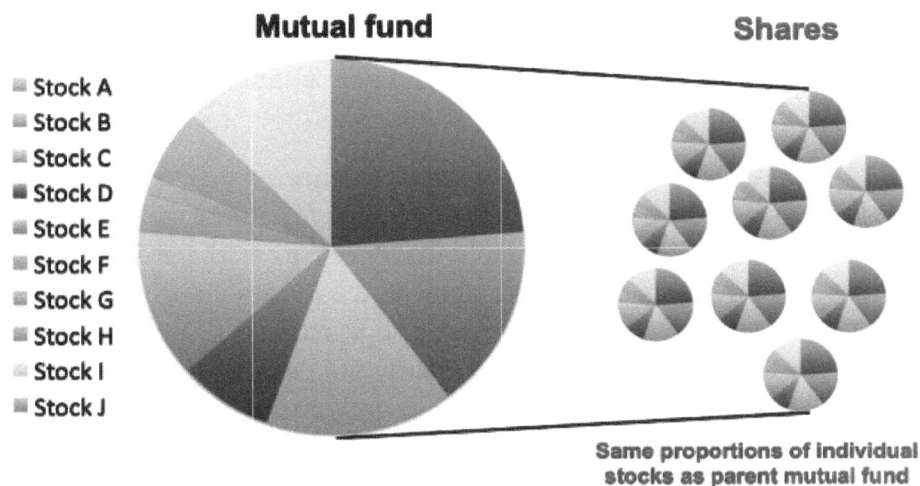

Figure 3. Investors who purchase shares of mutual funds will acquire stock portfolios with the same allocation as the parent mutual fund.

Another important concept involves the portfolio turnover, or changes in stock holdings resulting from the manager buying and selling at periodic intervals. Individual stocks that comprised the Massachusetts Investors Fund in 1930 are vastly different than today due to the natural evolution of businesses in our world. In fact, several of the stocks in its 1930 portfolio ended up as failures while the mutual fund still stands strong in 2019. This illustrates a major benefit of mutual funds in that professionals manage the buying and selling of stocks for you. Large financial institutions have successful funds that can withstand the test of time to evolve along with the business landscape. For these reasons, investing beginners should allocate their stock holdings to low cost mutual funds while they're studying and learning about the growth of individual stocks. Investment firms such as Vanguard, Fidelity, TD Ameritrade or Schwab, among others, have a variety of funds that track the performance of a certain index such as the S&P500. The fees for owning these types of funds are taken from quarterly dividends and are generally less than 0.4%, or $40 for every $10,000 invested. This cost is much cheaper than what a portfolio manager charges, allowing for more of your dividends to be used for repurchasing new shares or pieces of the fund.

Online investment brokerage accounts can be opened in a few minutes and linked to your bank account for monetary transactions. Purchasing a mutual fund usually requires an initial investment of $1,000-$5,000. Thereafter, you can buy shares in $50 or $100 increments. Thus, all it takes to start investing in mutual funds is a few thousand dollars. Many successful investors contribute a fixed amount to their funds every month. This is termed **dollar cost averaging** and is beneficial not only for beginners, but also for seasoned veterans of investing. The alternatives to dollar cost averaging are 1) investing a lump sum all at once, or 2) not investing. The advantages of investing are explained in **Chapter 1**, but why is dollar cost averaging better than investing a lump sum? The first obvious answer is that is takes time for most people to accumulate lumps to invest. Let's take the example of someone who saves $2000 a month and wants to contribute $50,000 to an investment account. Waiting to accumulate the entire $50,000 will take 25 months. This period of time could represent an opportunity loss for the individual if the savings are in a bank account earning 2% interest per year. At the end of 25 months, his or her savings will amount to $51,000. On the other hand, let's say another person buys a mutual fund that tracks the performance of the S&P500 stock market index. It will take 2 months for them to save enough money for the initial $3,000 minimum purchase. Once the fund is purchased, additional shares worth $2,000 are purchased every month. Importantly, funds tracking the S&P500 index are expected to increase by an average of 10% per year (some years will be better than others). By the end of 25 months, this account is likely to be worth $55,000, nearly 8% more than the person who waited to acquire $50,000 before purchasing. Therefore, dollar cost averaging can be a beneficial investment strategy to increase the value of your portfolio over time.

Another advantage of dollar cost averaging is realized whenever the market is in a downturn and underperforming, resulting in your stocks losing value based on their share prices. Market fluctuations are a natural part of stock market cycles. Although prices generally go up over time, it is not possible to predict what will happen in the short term (days, months, 1-5 years). Therefore, people who invest using a lump sum method would be at a greater risk of losing value *IF* the stock market suddenly takes a downward spiral. Let's take the previous example and flip it around. Person A has $50,000 invested in a low cost mutual fund tracking the S&P500. Person B will invest $2,000 per month for 25 months. During these 25 months, the S&P steadily decreases in value by 20%. At the end of 25 months, person A will have a portfolio worth $41,000 while person B's portfolio would be worth $45,000, or 10% more than person A due to dollar cost averaging. This is because Person B was able to buy more shares at a lower cost compared to the $50,000 worth of shares that person A bought in the beginning. Now let's say that over the next 12 months, the market rebounds by 30%. This is not an unlikely situation since the U.S. stock market has always rebounded to new highs following a recession. Person's B's portfolio would then be worth $6,000 more than person A's. If these funds are forgotten and sit in the investment account for the next 10 years, then Persons A and B would have portfolio values worth $144,000 and $158,000, respectively. Thus, it pays to dollar cost average not only for beginners, but also for experienced investors.

U.S. versus the World
The United States has some of the largest and most successful companies in the world. To reflect this, your portfolio should contain a potent dose of American stocks. The reason is simple and can be explained in a few words: American stocks have historically outperformed those of other countries on a consistent

basis. To exemplify this, let's analyze the representative funds sold by Vanguard. The international fund VGTSX contains over 6,000 holdings including Nestle, Alibaba, Samsung and Royal Dutch Shell among many others. The one representing U.S. stocks is VFINX, which performs equivalent to the S&P 500 index minus the low managerial fee of 0.14% (which is deducted from quarterly dividends). Therefore, VFINX is composed of approximately 500 companies including Apple, Johnson & Johnson, Exxon Mobil, Wells Fargo, etc. Since the turn of the millennium, an investment in the American VFINX fund has nearly tripled, while the international VGTSX fund has only doubled in value, lagging behind American companies. This does not mean international stocks never take the lead, as they outperformed the U.S. for a span of 9 years ending in 2009. Prior to the financial crisis, at the end of 2007, the international fund had gained over 70% in value since January 1, 2000. Although this return is not mind blowing, it fared much better than the paltry 11% return of VFINX from 2000-2007. After the financial crisis ended in 2009, however, it was America's time to shine. A 10-year investment in VFINX starting on January 1, 2009 more than tripled in value, while VGTSX only increased by 80% during this time frame. Investors who weathered both of the recessional storms in 2000 and 2008 saw their investment finally break even in 2011. Thus, most of the financial gains in individual portfolios from this time frame have occurred since 2011. This information illustrates two important points: first is that American stocks generally outperform international stocks over long periods of time. Second is there can be a tremendous amount of volatility in shorter stretches of 10 years or less. During these volatile periods, there is potential for international mutual funds to outperform the U.S. Therefore, ***your balance of American versus non-American funds should reflect your investing timeline.*** Money intended for long-term investments of 10 years or more can be used to purchase VFINX, or an equivalent fund tracking the S&P 500 index. Money intended for shorter-term investments of less than 10 years should be a mix of both American and international funds. The exact ratio is up to the individual investor, but should not be more than 50% international since the U.S. is known to outperform foreign stocks most of the time. While it is not possible to predict the future behavior of stock markets, learning from the past allows you to make powerful decisions that impact your future millionaire status.

Does size matter for investing?

Investors have hundreds of options to choose from regarding mutual funds. While some funds provide broad exposure to the market, such as VFINX and VGTSX described above, others are more focused on certain types of companies. In general, companies can be categorized by their size or type of business. The term "market capitalization (cap)" is often used to describe the size of a company. Simply put, the **market cap** is the number of publicly owned shares multiplied by the stock price. The number of shares available for trading is not fixed and often changes from year-to-year whenever companies either buy back shares or issue more for public trading. Ironically, increasing the number of shares available for trading is considered to decrease the intrinsic value of individual shares due to a corresponding decrease in earnings per share. Over time, this can result in decreased stock prices. On the other hand, companies that purchase their own shares decrease the number available for public trading, resulting in an increased intrinsic value per share. Due to fluctuations in the number of outstanding shares and stock prices, market capitalization changes on a daily basis. As a rule of thumb, giant companies have a market cap greater than $200 billion, large companies are $10-$200 billion, medium companies are $2-$10 billion, small companies are $0.3-$2 billion, and micro companies are less than $300 million. Some mutual funds are composed of company stocks that correspond to a certain size, or cap. By focusing investments on only one category, individuals are hoping to beat the total market average over time. Once again, while it is impossible to predict the future, we can learn from the history of stock prices. The following analysis explores the value of mutual fund investing by company size, or market cap.

By definition, successful companies are able to grow very large and survive many years. Therefore, giant capitalization stocks are a mainstay of investing and significantly contribute to the portfolio of many mutual funds. Also by definition, giant companies have less room to grow in the future due to an upper limit on the number of new customers available for their business product(s). One reason that people enjoy investing in giant companies is the large dividend payment received four times a year. Dividends are guaranteed income that individuals must pay taxes on in non-retirement accounts. Most investors who still need to save for retirement will reinvest quarterly dividends into more shares of the company or mutual fund. By doing so, they trust that stock prices will increase over time to make those additional shares more valuable. This fact does not necessarily mean that mutual funds composed of giant companies will have large dividend payouts because the fund managers will exercise their discretion for reinvesting the dividends into more shares. Over long periods of time (greater than 10 years), mutual funds composed of giant companies have paid investors quite well. An example of this is the TIAA Large Cap Growth Fund (symbol TILGX). This is primarily composed of U.S. stocks from giant companies such as Microsoft, Amazon, Mastercard and Apple. In addition, large companies constitute one-third of the overall portfolio. TILGX has outperformed the S&P 500 fund TISPX by 24% over the last 13 years, demonstrating that bigger is better. However, there have been times in 2006, 2016 and 2017 when TISPX outperformed TILGX. Therefore, most of your long-term investment money should be in giant/large cap mutual funds, while short-term investments can be allocated to mutual funds tracking the S&P500. It is important to note that even S&P500 funds are primarily composed (>80%) of giant and large companies. The difference is that TILGX and comparable funds are almost entirely (>90%) giant/large companies.

What about medium-cap funds? These include a very diverse group of businesses that may significantly increase, decrease or remain stagnant over time. Therefore, medium cap funds are less predictable and more subject to cyclical variation than giant/large cap funds. Accordingly, the portfolio turnover of mutual funds tend to increase as their market cap decreases. While fund managers attempt to only purchase successful companies, it is not possible to predict the future of medium-cap stocks due to several variables that are unknown to the public. This includes company plans for growth, downsizing, competition and future sales. Rather than paying dividends, profits may be spent on expanding a department, creating and marketing new products or maybe even increasing the salary of chief executives. In addition, companies that grow to a market cap of greater than $10 billion are no longer considered medium-sized and must be sold by the fund in order to remain consistent with its investing objectives. It is important to know that giant companies have all gone through their adolescent medium-cap phase of life. You may recall the volatility of your adolescent years and different trajectories that your life could have taken by many small decisions, opportunities or serendipity. The same is true for medium-cap stocks. While individual stocks in this category are not for the faint of heart, mutual fund that are composed of medium-sized companies are more predictable due to their broader market exposure with hundreds of individual stocks. Over the 12 years from 2002-2014, the TIAA Mid Cap Value Fund TIMVX outperformed the S&P 500 fund TISPX by 53%! This was due to the better growth potential of medium-cap stocks compared to large cap. However, adolescents are sometimes known to ignore their chores or behave irresponsibly. With this concept applied to mutual funds, erratic behavior can result in under performance for certain periods of time. Considering the random individual stocks within our investment universe, the behavior of any large cap stock is generally more predictable than a medium cap stock. During the five year span from 2014-2019, TIMVX actually underperformed TISPX by 21%. Therefore, medium cap investing is recommended for long time frames of 10 or more years.

The same can be said for small- and micro-sized companies. Like new plants germinating from seeds, small companies have the potential to grow enormously if provided the proper resources and care in their environment, eventually providing an endless supply of fruit for their investors to enjoy forever. As any gardener knows, most of the seeds that we plant do not flourish. Thus, gardeners will sow many more seeds than are needed and then thin plants as the strongest ones begin to grow. To accommodate this uncertainty from an investing standpoint, small cap fund managers will purchase tens or perhaps even hundreds of small cap stocks for their portfolio. For example, the TIAA-Cref Small Cap Equity Fund (TISEX) consists of approximately 360 stocks. Over a 10-year span from 2004-2014, this fund outperformed its older sister tracking the S&P 500, TISPX, by 10%. From 2014-2019, however, TISEX underperformed TISPX by 8.5%, demonstrating the cyclical behavior of small cap funds compared to the gold standard S&P 500 index. One reason for this propensity of small cap funds for over- and under-performance is their tendency towards exaggerated responses to market fluctuations. Thus, small cap funds tend to outperform during bull markets and under-perform during bear markets. Although not a general rule of thumb, this trend has been somewhat consistent over the last 15 years. For this reason, small cap mutual funds should primarily be purchased for long-term investing, similar to medium cap funds.

Using Momentum to Your Advantage

As mentioned above, certain types of mutual funds will over- or under-perform the S&P 500 index periodically, so how do you decide on which fund to purchase? One method uses the principle of momentum. Many people have yet to realize that the universal nature of Sir Isaac Newton's First Law of Thermodynamics also applies to mutual fund investing: Paraphrased, "An object in motion stays in motion until acted on by external forces." This suggests that funds doing well right now will probably continue to do well until investor sentiment or the economic climate changes. This has implications for individuals who dollar cost average in no-load (no-fee) mutual funds. Every few months you can evaluate the performance of funds that specialize in certain assets and invest in the one performing the best over the short term. Let's use TIAA as an example of a financial institution that allows people to manage their own retirement accounts. There has been a trend for large cap stocks to outperform other classes. During the first 3 months of 2019, the TILGX fund increased in value by nearly 20 percent while the small cap fund TISEX increased by 17 percent. Based on this recent performance, paycheck contributions during April of that year should have been allocated to TILGX. This strategy takes into account the universal nature of Isaac Newton's First Law. Remember that a certain portion of your investments should be allocated to bonds. Therefore, investors recognizing the power of momentum invested approximately 87% of their paycheck retirement contributions to TILGX or an equivalent fund in April 2019, with 13% invested in more stable bond funds. Now let's consider another period of time: the three months starting January 1, 2009 saw a decline in stock prices, with most stock funds losing money. Investors recognizing this trend will allocate all of their paycheck contributions to their favorite bond fund with more or less guaranteed rates of return. Then when the market recovers by showing an overall trend towards growth based on its recent 3 month performance, the entire portfolio should be rebalanced in order to achieve the predetermined asset allocation of bonds and stocks (13/87%), as explained earlier. An advantage of this strategy is the ease with which you can track the performance of mutual funds rather than individual stocks, which are more volatile in short periods of time.

WTF are ETFs?

Excitement is an important element for any relationship. For some people, this includes their relationship with investing. While the performance of mutual funds are reliable, dependable and more or less predictable in relation to stock market behavior, these qualities are not sufficient to maintain the interest of every type of investor. To spice things up, you can purchase **Ex**change-**T**raded **F**unds, abbreviated **ETF**s. Purchasing shares of an ETF is the same process as purchasing shares of a stock; however, ETF portfolios are similar to that of mutual funds in that they consist of a collection of stocks that track an index such as the S&P500. One attractive quality of an ETF is the flexibility with which investors have for selling shares. While mutual funds often require a holding period of 60 days or more before they can be sold, ETFs can be purchased and sold in the same day, similar to stocks. While selling shares is not recommended as a long-term investment strategy, this illustrates the hybrid nature of ETFs as having characteristics of both mutual funds and stocks. Further, the price of ETFs fluctuates throughout the day similar to stocks, while mutual funds can only be purchased after the markets close each day. Overall, the variety of ETFs offered is similar to that of mutual funds. Another potential advantage of ETFs is that you can start investing with lower sums of money. For instance, mutual funds may require a $1,000-$5,000 initial investment. On the other hand, you can purchase a few hundred dollars worth of ETFs. If you are a newbie making your first investment, make sure that you account for the brokerage transactions fees when making purchases, as these fees are largely what keep brokerages in business. For example, if you buy $100 worth of an ETF and pay a $5 transaction fee, your investment must increase by 5% before you break even. Therefore, you must be prepared to hold your ETF for at least one year before expecting any type of return on investment. On the other hand, purchasing $10,000 worth of an ETF still carries the same $5 transaction fee. Compared to the size of your investment, the transaction fee is a negligible 0.05% in this case and you would start to see a return on investment when the portfolio gains just 0.06%. During bull markets, this could happen within just a few days.

ETFs on Steroids

People who are very optimistic about the potential of ETFs to produce capital gains within a specified time frame may purchase **triple-leveraged ETFs**. These are funds with price activity that moves in the same direction as their equivalent portfolios, but at triple the magnitude. An example of a triple-leveraged ETF is the Direxion Daily S&P500 Bull 3X shares, or SPXL. Whenever the S&P500 has a great day and gains 1%, the SPXL fund in turn gains approximately 3%. Due to its expense ratio, the magnitude of the gain for SPXL will not be exactly 3%. Nevertheless, this price action produces mega returns for investors during a bull market. Consider the long bull market from January 30, 2009 to September 28, 2018. A $1,000 investment in the S&P500-tracking fund SPY would have grown into $3,500, a very good performance for any 9-year span. However, the same $1,000 invested in SPXL would have ballooned into $23,000- over 6 times more than the S&P500 fund! Therefore, triple-leveraged ETFs are guaranteed to outperform the market... when it's going up. On the other hand, their volatile nature causes them to be extremely risky for hold long-term holding. Consider working for a boss who can be very pleasant on good days or a bear to deal with on not-so-good days. You will feel rewarded to work with him and be part of the team when things are going well. During tough times, however, you could feel like a total loser to be associated with him. The same can be said for tripled-leveraged ETFs. When the market decreases by 1%, the SPXL fund will decrease by 3%. During a bear market, this will compound into huge losses over a short period of time. For example, after September 28, 2018, the market decreased for the remainder of the year. A $1,000 investment in the S&P500 would have diminished to $850, while the same $1,000 invested in SPXL would have diminished to a paltry $600, or 30% worse than the S&P500 in just 3 months! While the market tends to go up over time, it takes a while to recover losses. To get back to the original $1,000 starting point, the S&P500 fund had to gain nearly 18% from its low price, while the SPXL fund would had to gain 67%. Therefore, after such a substantial decline in the stock market, it could take much longer to recover losses from the triple leveraged fund. The possible short-term benefits of owning these funds must be weighed against the risk of a short-term stock market collapse. It is recommended for investors who are fortunate enough to acquire capital gains with triple leveraged funds to periodically sell and use the money to purchase a regular S&P 500 fund, as this action would then guarantee that the capital gains you sold will end up outperforming the stock market starting from the day you originally purchased the triple-leveraged fund. Then, whenever you feel confident that the market has nowhere to go but up, the funds can be used to repurchase SPXL shares.

CHAPTER 4

Stock investing

After congratulating yourself for deciding to plunge into stock purchases, what do you actually do? A few steps must be taken between your decision and a lifetime forecast of the legendary money rain that so few know about. First, open an online brokerage account. Second, buy stocks. Third, wait for the rain. This simple strategy is confounded by the sheer plethora of stocks in the vast market sea. Picking them can seem like a blinded fishing expedition, and it is unless you have a strategy for choosing the type and diversity of companies that give your hard earned money the best opportunity for growth. Thousands of publicly traded companies exist, but choosing them is quite different than processes people use for picking lottery numbers. For instance, purchasing stocks based on your favorite words, initials or abbreviations is likely to be a losing strategy, whereas this may work in the long-term for lottery players. For one thing, a lottery ticket is cheap whereas investors typically devote a larger portion of their income to stock purchases. In addition, lottery drawings happen frequently whereas it takes significantly more time for good stocks to grow in value. Once you make the decision to invest rather than gamble your money, you will then look to achieve certain qualities in not only stock holdings but also portfolio structure. The previous chapter on mutual fund investing may be sufficient for many readers; however, stock investing offers some advantages over mutual funds. First, good stocks grow much faster than standard S&P500-tracking mutual funds, with a few examples including Apple (AAPL), Amazon (AMZN) and Netflix

(NFLX). Investing in these companies during their infancy led to substantial gains in short spans of time (10 years or less). Second, there are no fees for holding a stock, whereas mutual funds charge nominal fees for managing the fund. Third, stocks can be traded any time of the day whereas mutual funds are only traded after the close of business. Fourth, stocks can be traded at a higher frequency than mutual funds, which may require a holding period of 60 days. Fifth, stocks may be more tax-efficient, as share prices will increase tax-free until they are sold. Sixth, some stocks pay much higher dividends than S&P500 funds while still giving investors an opportunity for growth of share prices over time.

Since mutual funds are professionally managed, they can be a good place to start looking for your first stocks to purchase. As described in **Chapter 3**, mutual funds may track the S&P500 or some other index that focuses on certain types of businesses. These businesses may be categorized by size, service, product, geographical location, or any combination of these. By glancing at the portfolio of your favorite mutual fund, you will see which companies are most heavily represented. By evaluating performance, you will no doubt see that some companies perform better than others over certain periods of time. *Each stock was purchased by the portfolio manager because it was perceived to have the potential to either grow or provide a stable source of income.* This chapter provides guidance on becoming your own portfolio manager by detailing certain qualities such as size, revenue and dividends.

Cap size

While more complex than ordering French fries, anyone's investment appetite can be satisfied with the many options for purchasing stocks ranging in cap size from mega, large, medium, small to micro. Here, cap is an abbreviation for **market capitalization**, meaning the total worth of publicly traded shares. For instance, at the time of this writing McDonald's stock (MCD) has 764 million shares available for trading on public markets. Multiplied by the share price of $194, this equals a market cap of about $148 billion, qualifying it as a large cap stock. As you can tell from this simple equation, cap size is determined by only two variables: numbers of shares outstanding and price per share. In order for it to grow into a mega size company, the number of MCD shares either has to increase to 1.1 billion, or the current share price has to increase to $270. This would result in a market cap over $200 billion, the lower limit for mega size companies. While everyone seems to have a daily limit for consuming French fries, too much of a good thing is desirable in the investment world. Remember that mega companies all started small in their beginning- perhaps in someone's garage or kitchen. Over time, most companies go out of business for one reason or another, but a select few will blossom into some of the largest and most well known companies in the world. Although companies can technically increase their market cap by increasing their number of shares, in reality it really has to do with share price. This is ultimately determined by sales, revenue, profits and speculation. Let's say that a certain company selling for $100 decides to increase its number of publicly available shares by 20% from 1 million to 1.2 million. This is termed a **share dilution** and does not actually increase the market cap in the long run. If companies are like a cake, then share dilutions result in more pieces being cut, but the size of the cake remains the same (**Fig. 4**). The reason is because a company's size ultimately depends on how much money the business is making. If each share has an intrinsic value of $100, then the above mentioned share dilution would result in each share being worth $80 with all other things being equal. Business revenues are reported to the public as **Earnings Per Share (EPS)**, which would decrease in response to share dilutions. Upon viewing this information, investors respond by paying less money for each stock to compensate for the share dilution. On the other hand, companies sometimes buy back their own shares, which will eventually increase EPS numbers, followed by stock prices. As you can see, the most important way for individual companies to increase their cap size is to make more money. Investors respond to positive business reports by flocking more and more money into successful companies. Over time, companies will expand their business, possibly acquire smaller businesses and ultimately grow into large and mega cap sizes. Therefore, if you can identify a small company today that will metamorphosize into a mega company within 15 years, you will end up earning millions on your initial investment. In reality, it is difficult to identify small companies that are destined to become mega. Let's face it- predicting anything to happen 10-15 years down the road is difficult. Therefore, most investors allocate a substantial portion of their assets to large and mega companies since they have typically stood the test of time and proven to be successful. In addition, a smaller portion of assets are typically allocated towards medium-sized and small companies, with hopes that they will blossom into large companies within the next few years.

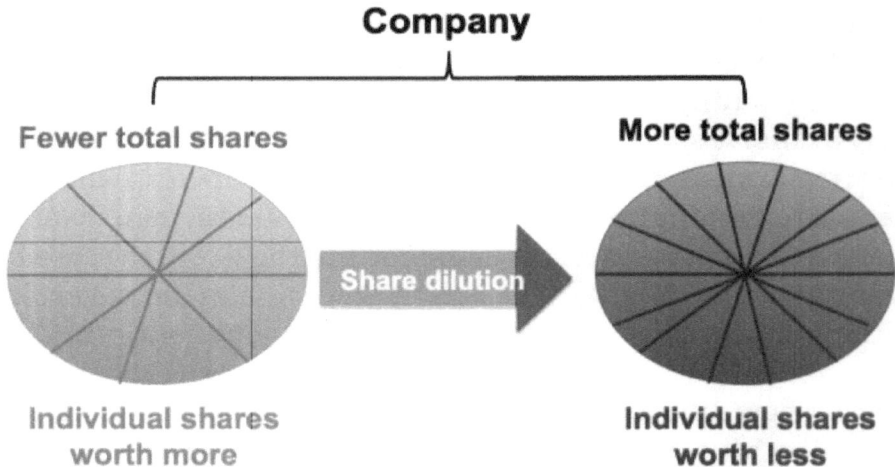

Figure 4. Company share dilutions result in lower intrinsic values for individual shares because they represent a smaller fraction of the total company.

Another advantage of mega companies is that many pay out a portion of their revenues to investors in the form of dividends. Once you become rich, this will provide an important source of your income. As investors, dividends are part of the company profits that belong to you, and you will notice that share prices decrease by the same amount as the dividend payout. For example, a company that trades at $100 per share may issue a quarterly dividend (every 3 months) of $0.50. After the dividend is distributed, share prices drop to $99.50. Since the annual dividend payout is $2/share ($0.50 x 4), anyone who purchases the stock at $100 would receive an annual 2% payout in cash on the investment. If you happen to own 50,000 shares, then your income from this investment would be $100,000/year. Most individuals can live comfortably on this amount. In addition, your balance of 50,000 shares remains constant and has the potential to increase in value. As you know, stock prices will fluctuate quite a bit. Therefore, if the same company fell to $90/share at some point but still paid $0.50 quarterly dividends, then the dividend payout of your investment would be 2.2% annually for all shares purchased at $90. Some large companies are well known for increasing dividend payouts on a regular basis. For example, AT&T (symbol T) has increased its dividend by at least 1 cent every year since 1998. This is a sign of a stable company that can be used as a source of income for stock holders; however, growth will be limited since profits are paid to stock holders rather than being reinvested for company growth. At current prices in 2019, AT&T's dividend payout is 5% per year, which means that $100 worth of stock will pay you $5 per year in dividend income. If you're a high roller, then $1 million worth of AT&T stock will give you $50,000 in annual income. Not bad for sitting at home and doing nothing. In addition, you can be fairly confident that next year AT&T will increase it's dividend payout even more. This knowledge can especially play into your favor during recessions, as T stock even increased its dividends during the 2000 and 2008 fiascoes. After 2008, for example, T stock went down to the $25 range prior to its recovery back up to $40. Therefore, shareholders who bought it at this price were receiving a 6% dividend payout at a time when many people were nervous about investing. Dividend stocks such as AT&T can be very valuable for individuals who have already acquired their fortune. Owning these types of stocks is particularly useful during recessions when the reliable dividend payouts can be reinvested at low share prices or saved as cash. On the other hand, acquiring a fortune in the first place will depend more heavily on companies that do not pay large dividends, but rather reinvest their profits towards growth and expansion. In this respect, mega companies that pay less than the 1.8% average of the S&P500 in dividends will offer greater probabilities for capital appreciation as long as their revenues continue increasing.

The greatest stock growth, however, happens when people who purchase a small cap company (<$2 billion market cap) get lucky watching it balloon into a large cap over time. Let's examine Netflix (symbol NFLX). Anyone could have purchased this stock for $2 per share back in 2005. In other words, a $1000 investment would have gotten you 500 shares. At the time of this writing, NFLX has a $120 billion market cap and is trading at $286 a share. This means someone who made the original $1000 investment would now have 500 shares of stock that is collectively worth $143,000! This example illustrates that small companies that end up becoming very successful will give you the greatest opportunity to get rich. This is much more difficult than it sounds, as finding a good small cap company may be every bit as serendipitous as finding a needle in a haystack. In addition, if NFLX had paid dividends during their early years, the company would not have had enough funds to expand to the level it has. Businesses are able to grow by reinvesting their profits back into the business. It is feasible to think that once Netflix has maximized its growth opportunities in the future, it will start paying out dividends to investors. Owning a balanced portfolio of mega, large, medium and small-cap stocks will allow you to reap the benefits of partnering with some of the most successful and stable companies in the world, while also allowing you to potentially find the next Netflix. Beginners should start by investing in the largest companies, and then move towards smaller market cap stocks as they become more confident. An aggressive portfolio may consist of 30% mega, 25% large, 20% medium, 15% small and 10% consisting of bonds, cash or annuity funds. Notice that at any one time, most of your money should be invested in mega and large cap stocks, as these companies have the biggest influence on stock market performance.

CHAPTER 5

Using retirement accounts to your advantage

Why even mention retirement accounts if the whole point of this book is the get rich and not have to work to an old age? This question is justified, as retirement accounts are typically used for income after the age of 60, and you will want to stop working before then. The majority of people in the United States who are healthy, hard workers and disciplined investors should never have to work to an old age given our ample opportunities for employment, education and investing in the world's most successful companies. The myth that people should continue to work until age 60 or 70 was in part facilitated by the Social Security program, resulting in a mandatory 6% paycheck deduction to pay the current generation of retirees, who supported the previous generation and so on. This system encourages us to work this long because that's what previous generations did and it's necessary to maintain the system. The outdated Social Security retirement program functions like an annuity, in which monthly paychecks progressively increase as long as you postpone your benefits until your "full retirement age" of 67. Although collecting social security benefits as "early" as age 62 may be useful, people who read this book in their 30's will not depend on the program for retirement income. Rather, this chapter will help you to realize that other types of accounts (Roth IRA, Roth 403b, 457b) will actually *FACILITATE* early retirement. In addition, these vehicles will also help to prevent you from running out of money in your 60's and 70's. Therefore, this author believes that social security contributions (as well as its deferred benefits) should be optional rather than mandatory since we now have much better and more versatile individual retirement plans at our disposal. Although discussing the pros and cons of Social Security is outside the scope of this book, you can imagine the impact of investing an additional 6% of your salary over the course of your working life.

IRAs (Traditional, Roth)

The first thing you should do after reading this sentence is to open an Individual Retirement Account (IRA), or thank the IRA that you already have. You should thank it for all the benefits it will provide you in your retirement days. If you are a newbie to investing, you should stash $6,000 into your new IRA each year before utilizing other investment accounts. The reason is because IRAs are tax-advantaged. That's right, they give ordinary people the kind of tax break that you typically associate with uber wealthy individuals. When you open an IRA, you will be asked if you want the Traditional or Roth variety. The difference is that income deposited into Traditional IRAs is not taxed by the IRS until you withdraw it after turning 60. Let's say that you have an annual income of $50,000 and contribute $6,000 of it to a Traditional IRA. When you file your taxes the next year, you will receive credit for this contribution and only be taxed on $44,000 of your income. This sounds advantageous, but remember that money you have in a Traditional IRA must remain there until you turn 60. On the other hand, income deposited into Roth accounts is taxed as normal, but withdrawals after the age of 60 are tax-free. Young people reading this will choose the Roth type because investments that have a long time to grow typically will. You heard it right- the capital gains, equity and dividends will be collected tax free after turning 60! This is not the only advantage, as your contributions to Roth accounts can be withdrawn whenever without any penalty. For instance, let's say you invest $6,000 into a Roth IRA for two years, but then have a medical emergency costing $10,000. You can technically withdraw all of your contributions (up to $12,000 in this example). However, capital gains cannot be withdrawn until age 60 unless you agree to pay a massive 10% penalty. On the other hand, all contributions that are withdrawn from a Traditional IRA before the age of 60 are subject to the penalty. Therefore, you should favor a Roth IRA because you want to retire early and have it provide some income when you are young enough to enjoy. In addition, Roth IRAs will provide you with long-term capital gains when you turn 60. A 30 year old who invests $6,000 a year and retires at age 50 will be able to withdraw the total of her contributions ($120,000). The remaining money would have to wait another 10 years before it can be withdrawn without penalty. Keep in mind that a $120,000 withdrawal would not drain the account at all, as it would be worth over half a million dollars by age 50. On the other hand, $120,000 is not enough for a person to live on between ages 50 and 60. *Therefore, you must have additional sources of income besides a Roth IRA if you want to retire early.*

(Roth) 403b

Another type of account to supplement your retirement savings is a Roth 403b. These are commonly offered by tax-exempt organizations such as schools. Similar to a Roth IRA, income that is deposited into a Roth 403b is taxed the next year while withdrawals beyond age 60 will be tax-free. The reason Roth 403b accounts are marvelous is that individuals may contribute $19,500 a year through paycheck deductions. Therefore, employers who offer Roth 403b accounts for retirement are your friend. This may be an important consideration when job hunting, and the information is typically available on their Human Resources website. Once employment is severed, funds from the Roth 403b may be rolled-over to your Roth IRA. Let's say that you work at a school and max out your 403b contributions for 10 years before leaving. You would have contributed $195,000 to it, of which you have already paid taxes. At this point, your account of approximately $270,000 is transferred to your Roth IRA. You then have $195,000 sitting there for you to withdraw and spend whenever it suits your fancy. Remember this is the money you've already paid taxes on. Meanwhile, the remaining $75,000 will sit in the account until you get old. The longer you work, the better off you are. Let's say that you max out Roth 403b contributions for 20 years so that your account is worth $800,000, of which nearly half ($390,000) would qualify as contributions. When you also consider your IRA contributions for those 20 years, this brings your total Roth contributions to $510,000! Even if you withdraw the entirety of your contributions, there would still be over $500,000 left in your Roth account, which would actually double over the next 7-10 years while you're waiting to turn 60 and can withdraw all of it tax-free. Therefore, the word Roth should always catch your eye and make your ears perk up. During your short time here on Earth, make sure that you maximize all of your Roth investment opportunities.

There is a disadvantage to Roth 403b accounts in that investments are limited to mutual funds rather than stocks. If you prefer mutual funds, than this is not an issue. In contrast, Roth IRAs usually have more investment choices and allow for stock purchases. If you really prefer to get your tax break now rather than waiting, then traditional 403b accounts are an alternative to the Roth type. These are similar to Traditional IRAs, in which taxes are deferred on the money you contribute. Therefore, if your salary is $100,000 per year and you contribute $19,500 to a traditional 403b, then your taxable income would be $80,500. Remember in this case that you would ultimately be taxed on all withdrawals upon retirement.

457

A third kind of retirement account offered to state or local government employees is called deferred compensation, or 457. It has similarities with the other accounts discussed earlier, such as having a Roth or Traditional format with an annual contribution limit of $19,500. The great thing about a 457 is that investors can withdraw funds without penalty at any time following employment. Traditional 457 owners will see their taxable income increase by the amount of the withdrawal. This illustrates the reason it's called "**deferred compensation**": employees have it deducted from their paycheck now in order for it provide a massive payday later. Whatever is left in your account grows tax-deferred (or tax-free for Roth accounts)! Due to the ability to withdraw funds without penalty, some would rank 457 plans as having a higher priority than 403b plans. Let's imagine you decide to contribute the maximum amount to each plan for 10 years: $195,000 to 403b, $195,000 to 457, and $60,000 to Roth IRA. At the end of 10 years, your total investments would be worth about $620,000. Not bad for someone who was broke to start with. It is easy to see how someone currently in this position is only 5 years away from millionaire status.

401

401 plans are the most common type of retirement account offered by employees. In these, employee contributions are matched by employers up to a certain percentage of salary, commonly 3-8%. Let's say that you landed a job paying $100,000/year. The company may allow you to contribute up to $6,000, or 6%, of your salary to the plan. Receiving a matching contribution from the company would result in your plan getting a total of $12,000 a year, equally spread out through each paycheck. The IRS allows employers to offer one of two different subtypes of 401 plans: "a" or "k." While both types of plans are similar, 401a is used by educational institutions while 401k is used by other types of companies. These are tax-advantaged funds which are intended to provide a portion of retirement income for employees who work for companies that do not offer a pension. In fact, over the last few decades 401 plans have largely replaced pensions in terms of retirement planning. One of the advantages is that employees have more control over their investments. This is good since your investment strategy in part depends on your time horizon: only you know when you will ride off into the sunset. It is very desirable for employees to contribute an amount to

their 401 plan that qualifies them to receive the maximum matching contribution from the company. The size of the company match may be one of the factors that helps you to determine who to work for: employers that offer an 8% company match to your salary are more desirable than companies offering a 3% match. For retirement planning, you may think about the company match as an addition to your base salary. For someone with a $100,000 salary and 8% company match, they are actually getting $108,000 per year. Some of this $108,000 is tax-advantaged while most of it is taxed. When saving for retirement, you will want to maximize your tax-advantaged accounts whether it's a Roth or Traditional type. When you turn 60 years old, you may start withdrawing funds from the 401 account penalty-free. If you want to retire early, then simply roll over your 401 funds into an IRA after leaving work so that you will have more control over them. Working for 15 years with a 8% company match in your 401 account will result in an account balance of roughly $400,000. Without the company match, it would only be half of that number. Therefore, contribute the amount of money that is necessary to receive the full company match. When you retire early, make sure there are enough funds in your 457 and Roth accounts to provide for your living expenses until you reach age 60. Then you can start using your 401 account without worrying about paying a 10% penalty on your withdrawals.

Let's visualize how you will maximize the benefits of all your retirement accounts. You start making bank ($100,000) at age 35 and the company offers 401, 403 and 457 plans. In addition, you make the full contribution to your IRA during this time. After 15 years, you are ready to leave the workforce forever!! Your Roth IRA will be worth $150,000, of which $90,000 are your contributions. Your Roth 403b with be worth $490,000, of which $292,500 are contributions. Your Traditional 457 plan is worth about the same, and 401 has banked a total of $300,000. In this scenario, your retirement accounts will be worth $1.4 million at age 50. The money available at your immediate disposal comes from all of your Roth contributions ($382,500) and 457 deferred compensation ($490,000) plans. You will live off of this $872,500 for 10 years until the money from your capital gains and 401 account become available. You decide to withdraw $70,000 a year to provide for your living expenses the next 10 years. This is an amount that many of us feel comfortable with. Note that withdrawing $70,000 a year will not deplete your account in a span of 10 years, as long as remaining funds stay invested in a portfolio allocation that averages 6% returns a year (50% bonds, 50% stocks). Therefore, you are not depleting your account or taking an unbalanced risk in the stock market. If $70,000 per year is not enough to make you comfortable, then you may want to work another year or two keeping your money invested at an 80:20 ratio of stocks and bonds to allow for more growth. If you decide to go ahead and retire, then you will have an additional $1 million available to you at age 60. Therefore, the total funds of all your accounts at age 60 will be $1.6 million. Keep in mind that you will also start collecting Social Security payments when you turn 62. If you want to retire at age 45 using this strategy, then you need to start saving at age 30. Overall, this plan assumes that you will maximize contributions to all of your retirement accounts for 15 years.

CHAPTER 6

From broke to millionaire plan in 15 years

Taking whatever money you have and multiplying it by one thousand would put you in a nice spot financially. This book is designed to make you visualize the process. It requires a considerable, concentrated and informed effort. First, you must have income that will support your desire to become a millionaire. Second, you must make sound investments. Third, hopefully you will get lucky with a good investment, but even if you don't make that lucky pick that rockets to the moon, you will be a position to accomplish your goal. Upon writing this, I reflect back to a time when I was broke. It did not feel good and negatively affected my emotional health and mental state of mind. At that time, investing was not a consideration because all of my money to was going to credit card companies, car dealerships and beer. After reading a little about investing including how people live on dividends, I realized that it takes years to get to that level, but it is doable. I was able to accomplish my goal of going from broke to millionaire in just over 14 years. The major driving force behind this was landing a job that paid nearly $100,000/year, allowing me to max out 401, 403b, 457b and Roth IRA contributions. If I was instead earning $60,000/year, then it would have taken 20 years to become a millionaire. Financial literacy is not common knowledge in our society, and once you are able to get out of debt and start the formidable task of saving, this book shows you the concrete steps to take and how to make informed decisions on your path to millionaire status. Since the company landscape is constantly changing, I do not recommend specific stocks, but encourage you to start with large cap mutual funds and study the companies responsible for their major movements. Then you can move on to studying small cap companies which may end up outperforming large cap stocks in the long run. It doesn't hurt to use 10% of your portfolio to try investing in the next Netflix- or Amazon-type stock during its infantile stage. If you are already 30 years old when reading this, then chances are you think that you feel old. On the other hand, following this strategy will still help you to retire early (age 50 or sooner). When examining this, you'll notice that your largest salary increases will come from job promotions or changing jobs. Remaining with the same job title only results in incremental salary increases. After you achieve your financial goals, you will realize that the first million takes the most effort and your money will double to $2 million in 7-8 more years. Without further ado I am pleased to share this plan for becoming millionaire within 15 years of today. Make sure you write down today's date when you read this, and you will see it come true.

Year 1
Job salary: $40,000
Roth IRA: $6,000
401 with company match: $4,000

Portfolio: 100% total stock market mutual fund

*Total funds: **$10,000***

Year 2: Get a promotion or new job
Job salary: $50,000
Roth IRA: $6,000
401: $6,000
457b: $3,000

Portfolio: 87/13 (Stocks/Bonds)

Total funds: $25,900

Year 3
Job salary: $54,000
Roth IRA: $6,000
401: $6,400
457b: $6,600

Portfolio: 87/13 (Stocks/Bonds)

Total funds: $47,200

Year 4
Job salary: $56,000
Roth IRA: $6,000
401: $6,700
457b: $8,300

Portfolio: 87/13 (Stocks/Bonds)

Total funds: $72,400

Year 5: Get a promotion or new job
Job salary: $65,000
Roth IRA: $6,000
401: $7,800
457b: $14,200

Portfolio: 87/13 (Stocks/Bonds)

Total funds: $107,000

Year 6
Job salary: $68,000
Roth IRA: $6,000
401: $8,100
457b: $17,900

Portfolio: 87/13 (Stocks/Bonds)

Total funds: $148,600

Year 7: Get a promotion or new job
Job salary: $85,000
Roth IRA: $6,000
401: $10,200
457b: $19,500
403b: $13,300

Portfolio: 87/13 (Stocks/Bonds)

Total funds: $212,000

Year 8
Job salary: $87,000
Roth IRA: $6,000
401: $10,400
457b: $19,500
403b: $16,000

Portfolio: 85/15 (Stocks/Bonds)

Total funds: $282,600

Year 9
Job salary: $88,000
Roth IRA: $6,000
401: $10,500
457b: $19,500
403b: $17,000

Portfolio: 85/15 (Stocks/Bonds)

Total funds: $360,500

Year 10
Job salary: $89,000

Roth IRA: $6,000
401: $10,600
457b: $19,500
403b: $17,900

Portfolio: 85/15 (Stocks/Bonds)

Total funds: $446,200

Year 11
Job salary: $90,000
Roth IRA: $6,000
401: $10,800
457b: $19,500
403b: $18,700

Portfolio: 80/20 (Stocks/Bonds)

Total funds: $538,700

Year 12
Job salary: $92,000
Roth IRA: $6,000
401: $11,000
457b: $19,500
403b: $19,500

Portfolio: 80/20 (Stocks/Bonds)

Total funds: $640,000

Year 13
Job salary: $93,000
Roth IRA: $6,000
401: $11,100
457b: $19,500
403b: $19,500
brokerage account: $900

Portfolio: 80/20 (Stocks/Bonds)

Total funds: $750,700

Year 14
Job salary: $94,000
Roth IRA: $6,000
401: $11,200
457b: $19,500
403b: $19,500
brokerage account: $800

Portfolio: 80/20 (Stocks/Bonds)

Total funds: $870,800

Year 15
Job salary: $95,000
Roth IRA: $6,000
401: $11,400
457b: $19,500
403b: $19,500
brokerage account: $600

Portfolio: 80/20 (Stocks/Bonds)

*Total funds: **$1,001,000***

Note that, depending on your lifestyle, you may be able to accomplish this feat with a final salary just under $100,000 per year. In addition, the earlier you are able to increase your salary, the better off you will be in the long run as long as you invest your raises. Start looking for opportunities today to put your broke self into a situation to become a millionaire within 15 years, and then follow-through with the advice presented here to build a legacy that your family and friends will be proud of.

www.ingramcontent.com/pod-product-compliance
Lightning Source LLC
Chambersburg PA
CBHW030539220526
45463CB00007B/2906